Contents

Introduction

1. Insight into the annual schedule
    - Training objectives
    - Annual schedule
    - Individual steps of the annual schedule
    - Creating well-structured training units

2. Structuring a training unit
    - Warm-up practices:
    - Basic exercises
    - Additional information on basic exercise
    - Basic play
    - Target play

3. Roles/tasks of the coach

4. Training units
    - Basics of the piston movement (★★)
    - Basics of the crossing movement (★★)
    - Interacting with the pivot (★★)
    - Long crossing of the center back and the wing player as initial action – Part 1 (★★★)
    - Long crossing of the center back and the wing player as initial action – Part 2 (★★★)
    - Long crossing of the center back and the wing player as initial action – Part 3 (★★★)

5. About the editor

6. Further reference books published by DV Concept

Publishing information
1st English edition released on 29 Sep 2018
German original edition released on 14 Jun 2014

Published by DV Concept
Editors, design, and layout: Jörg Madinger, Elke Lackner
Proofreading and English translation: Nina-Maria Nahlenz

ISBN: 978-3-95641-223-3

This publication is listed in the catalogue of the **German National Library**. Please refer to http://dnb.de for bibliographic data.

The work and its components are protected by copyright. No reprinting, photomechanical reproduction, storing or processing in electronic systems without the publisher's written permission.

1. Insight into the annual schedule

Training objectives
In the training of **adult teams**, a coach usually will be measured based on his or her success (league position). Hence, the individual training units are strongly focused on the respective opposing team (aim of season). Winning games and making efficient use of the team's potential are paramount.

In the training of **youth teams**, however, the **individual development** is the most important objective which has priority over success. The players should also be trained on a general basis, i.e. on each position (no positional specialization, no offense/defense specialization).

Annual schedule
The following points should be taken into consideration when creating your annual schedule:
- How many training units do I have (do not forget vacations, holidays, and the season schedule)?
- What do I want to achieve/improve this season?
- What goals should be achieved within a given concept (of the club, the association, i.e. the German Handball Association [DHB], for example)? You can refer to the publications of the DHB for information about defense systems, individual offense/defense skills, and the expected performance of a certain age group.
- What skills does my team have (do the individual players have)? You should continuously analyze and document the skills of your team so that you can make a target-performance comparison at a regular basis.

Introduction

Dear reader
Thank you for choosing a book of the handball-uebungen.de training guide series.

These training units elaborate initial actions against the 6-0 defense system as well as variable options for continued playing. The first three training units teach the tactical basics of playing against the 6-0 defense on an individual and a small-group basis. This includes the dynamic piston movement with breaking through decisions as well as the basics of crossing movements and team play with the pivot. The subsequent three training units introduce crossing of the center back with the wing player as an initial action and provide three more options for the team to overcome the defense through continued playing.

This book contains the following training units:

Basics of the piston movement (★★)
This training unit focuses on developing the basics of the piston movement. Following warm-up and a coordination run, the players develop the basics of the piston movement step by step during the subsequent ball familiarization and a piston movement team exercise. The goalkeeper warm-up shooting is characterized by piston movements/counter piston movements and a subsequent shot at the goal. In a small group exercise, the players further develop the piston movement, while the team exercise focuses on training the piston movement 5-on-5. A sprint contest completes this training unit.

Basics of the crossing movement (★★)
The objective of this training unit is to develop simple crossing moves. Following warm-up and a coordination run that includes reactions to changing situations, the players develop simple crossing moves during the ball familiarization exercise. In the subsequent goalkeeper warm-up shooting exercise, the crossing moves will be extended by a shot at the goal. Step by step, the players develop a crossing move with a subsequent shot from the back positions until finally, they are able to do two consecutive crossing moves. During the 6-on-6 final game, the players implement what they practiced before.

Interacting with the pivot (★★)
This training unit focuses on the interaction of the back position players with the pivot. Following a warm-up game and a ball familiarization exercise, the players practice the interaction with the pivot during the goalkeeper warm-up shooting. In the two subsequent exercises, the players further develop and practice the interaction step by step. A sprint contest completes this training unit.

Long crossing of the center back and the wing player as initial action – Part 1 (★★★)

This training unit focuses on the development of a simple initial action with crossing of the center back and the wing player. Following a short warm-up game, the players gradually develop the initial action during the ball familiarization phase. After the goalkeeper warm-up shooting, there are two team exercises during which the players practice the running moves of the initial action as well as several options for continued playing and variants. A closing game completes this training unit.

Long crossing of the center back and the wing player as initial action – Part 2 (★★★)

In this training unit, the players gradually further develop the initial action of the previous training unit and practice further possible solutions. Following a short warm-up game, the players develop the running paths during the ball familiarization phase. The goalkeeper warm-up shooting includes a simple crossing move with a subsequent shot at the goal. During two team exercises, the players practice the different playing options that are to be implemented in the subsequent closing game.

Long crossing of the center back and the wing player as initial action – Part 3 (★★★)

In this training unit, the players take up the initial action of the two previous training units and practice further possible solutions. Following warm-up with a coordination run, the players develop an additional crossing move during the ball familiarization exercise and the goalkeeper warm-up shooting. The players further develop this step by step in a series of shots. In a team exercise, the players combine the new crossing move with the initial action they practiced before and eventually implement both in a 6-on-6 game. A sprint contest completes this training unit.

Sample figure:

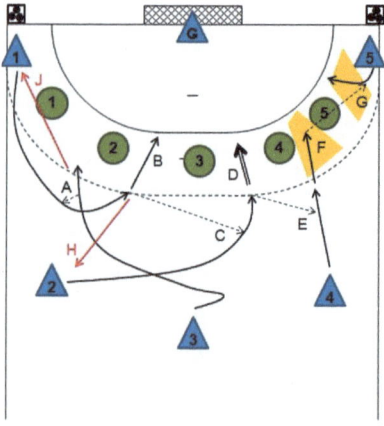

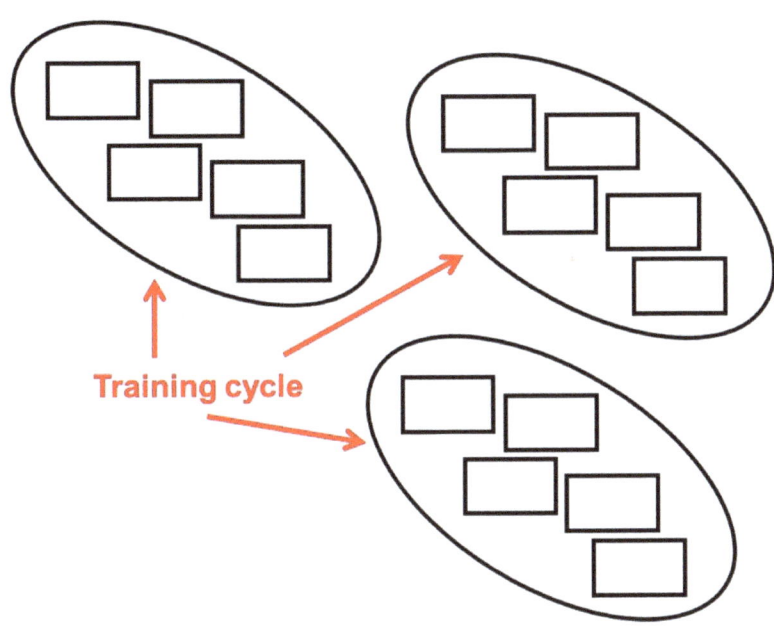

Individual steps of the annual schedule
A handball season can be divided into the following training phases:
- Preparatory phase until the first game: This phase is suitable for improving physical fitness skills such as endurance.
- 1st part of the season until the Christmas holidays: The Christmas break should be kept in mind here.
- 2nd part of the season until the end of season.

You should then refine and elaborate these training phases step by step.
- Division of training phases into sections with part-specific objectives (monthly schedule, e.g.).
- Division into weekly schedules.
- Planning of individual training units.

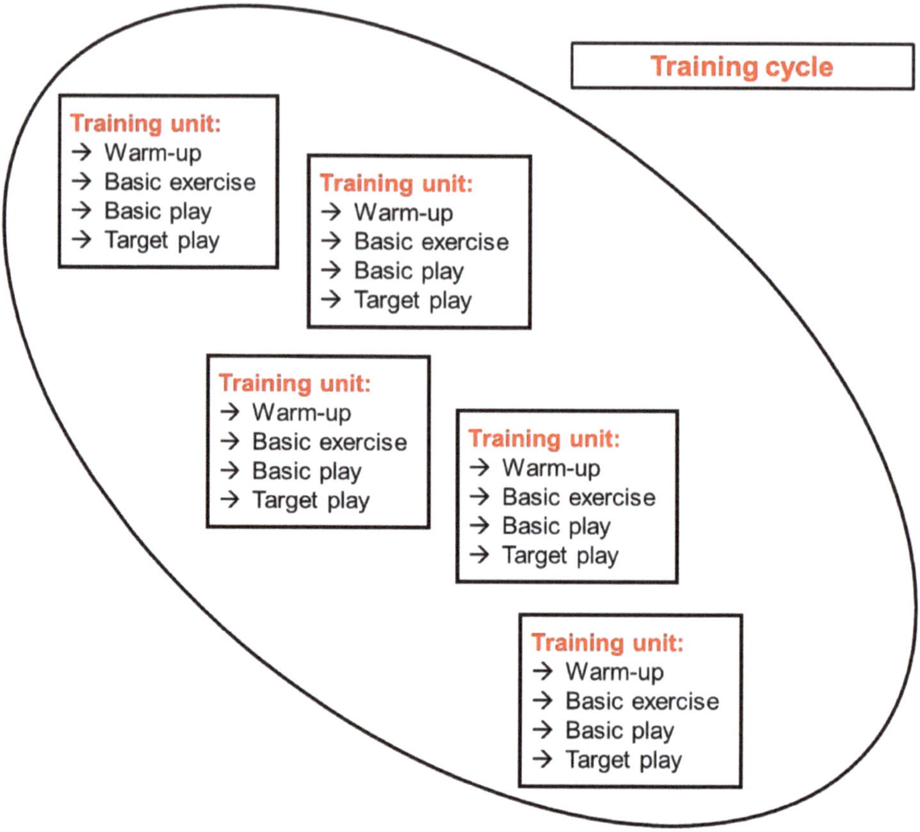

Training cycle

Training unit:
- → Warm-up
- → Basic exercise
- → Basic play
- → Target play

Training unit:
- → Warm-up
- → Basic exercise
- → Basic play
- → Target play

Training unit:
- → Warm-up
- → Basic exercise
- → Basic play
- → Target play

Training unit:
- → Warm-up
- → Basic exercise
- → Basic play
- → Target play

Training unit:
- → Warm-up
- → Basic exercise
- → Basic play
- → Target play

Creating well-structured training units

A clear structure is important for the annual schedule as well as for the planning of the individual training units.

- Work with parts (see monthly schedule). You should work on a special topic over a certain period of time, especially in the training of youth teams. That way, you can repeat exercises and make sure the players memorize the courses.
- Each training unit should have a clear training focus. Do not mix topics within a training unit, but make sure that each exercise has a well-defined objective.
- The players are corrected in accordance with the training unit's focus (when training the defense, defense actions are corrected and pointed out).

2. Structuring a training unit

The focus of the training should run like a red thread through the entire unit. It is advisable to follow the basic timescale below:
- Approx. 10 (15) minutes – warm-up.
- Approx. 20 (30) minutes – basic exercises (2 to 3 exercises max. plus goalkeeper warm-up shooting).
- Approx. 20 (30) minutes – basic play.
- Approx. 10 (15) minutes – target play.

1st timescale for a 60-minute training unit / 2nd timescale in brackets for a 90-minute training unit.

Warm-up practices
- Opening of the training unit: It may be advisable to start the training unit with a ritual (get together in a circle, exchanging high-fives) and to explain the contents and the objectives of the training unit to the players.
- Basic warm-up (jogging, activation of blood circulation and the musculoskeletal system).
- Stretching/strengthening/mobilization (preparing the body for the physical stress of the training unit).
- Short games (these should already focus on the objective of the training unit).

Basic exercises
- Ball familiarization (focused on the objective of the training unit).
- Goalkeeper warm-up shooting (focused on the objective of the training unit).
- Individual technique and tactics training.
- Technique and tactics training in small groups.

In general, the running and passing paths are predefined during the basic exercises (you may increase and vary the requirements during the course of the exercise).

Additional information on basic exercise
- Each player should do the drill (switch quickly).
- Very frequent repetitions.
- The players should rotate or do the drill on both sides simultaneously / slightly delayed to avoid long waiting periods.
- Practice individually (1-on-1 to 2-on-2 max.).
- Add additional tasks/drills, if applicable (to make the exercise more complex).

Basic play

Most of all, the basic play differs from the basic exercise in such a way that now there are several **options for action** (decisions). The player(s) should realize the respective options and make the ideal decision. Here, the players practice decision-making in particular.
- The players should now implement what they practiced during the basic exercises under **competitive conditions**.
- Working with alternative actions – practicing the decision-making process.
- The players should repeat the drill frequently and try out different actions.
- Working in small groups (3-on-3 to 4-on-4 max.).

Target play
- The players now implement what they practiced before in free play. To increase their motivation, you may award additional points or additional attacks for correct implementation.
- In the target play, the players implement what they practiced before (5-on-5, 6-on-6).

Depending on the contents and the objectives of the training unit, you may have to slightly adjust the timescales of the basic exercise and basic play (e.g. for endurance training where they may be substituted by endurance units).

Set topics
- Individual training of the players according to the respective conceptual training framework (DHB or the club's individual conceptual framework).
- Tactical training of defense and offense systems (age-dependent):
  - From man coverage to a 6-0 defense system, for example.
  - From 1-on1 to 6-on-6 with initial actions practiced in teams, for example.

Choose topic of training unit:
→ Red thread

Warm up:
Time:
- approx. 10 (15) minutes

Practices:
- "Playful warm-up"
- Games
- Coordination runs
- (Stretching and strengthening)

Basic exercise:
Time:
- approx. 20 (30) minutes

Characteristics:
- Individual/Small groups

Practices:
- Exact instructions re. course of the exercise
- Variants with exact instructions re. the course
- From simple to complex
- No waiting periods for players

Basic play:
Time:
- approx. 20 (30) minutes

Characteristics:
- Small groups

Practices:
- Exact instructions re. course
- Competition

Target play:
Time:
- approx. 10 (15) minutes

Characteristics:
- Team play (small groups)

Practices:
- Free play with the contents of the basic exercise and basic play
- Competition

3. Roles/tasks of the coach

It is mainly the personality and the behavior of the coach that makes the training a success. Therefore, it is important to observe certain behavioral rules to guarantee a successful training. The coach's social skills have an impact as important as his expertise.

A coach should:
- describe the training and its objectives to his team at the beginning of the training unit
- always speak loud and clear
- talk from such a position that all players can hear his instructions and corrections
- recognize and correct mistakes and give advice when correcting
- mainly correct what is part of the training objective
- point out and compliment on individual progress (give the player self-confidence)
- support and permanently challenge the players
- always be a role model - during training and games, but also outside the court
- come to training and games well-prepared and in a timely manner

Training unit requirements:

★	Simple requirement (all youth and adult teams)
★ ★	Intermediate requirement (youth teams under 15 years of age and adult teams)
★ ★ ★	Higher requirement (youth teams under 17 years of age and adult teams)
★ ★ ★ ★	Highest requirements (competitive area)

4. Training units

TU 1:		Basics of the piston movement		★★	90
Opening part		**Main part**			
X	Warm-up/Stretching		Offense/Individual		Jumping power
	Running exercise	X	Offense/Small groups	X	Sprint contest
	Short game	X	Offense/Team		Goalkeeper
	Coordination		Offense/Series of shots		
X	Coordination run		Defense/Individual	**Final part**	
	Strengthening		Defense/Small groups		Closing game
X	Ball familiarization		Defense/Team		Final sprint
X	Goalkeeper warm-up shooting		Athletics		
			Endurance		

Key:

✖ Cone

🔺 Attacking player

🟢 Defense player

▭ Small gym mat

▦ Ball box

▢ Small vaulting box

▯▯▯▯ Coordination ladder

Equipment required:
→ 1 coordination ladder, 2 small vaulting boxes, 8 cones, 4 small gym mats, ball box with sufficient number of handballs

Description:
This training unit focuses on developing the basics of the piston movement. Following warm-up and a coordination run, the players develop the basics of the piston movement step by step during the subsequent ball familiarization and a piston movement team exercise. The goalkeeper warm-up shooting is characterized by piston movements/counter piston movements and a subsequent shot at the goal. In a small group exercise, the players further develop the piston movement, while the team exercise focuses on training the piston movement 5-on-5. A sprint contest completes this training unit.

The training unit consists of the following key exercises:
- Warm-up/Stretching (individual exercise: 10 minutes/total time: 10 minutes)
- Coordination run (10/20)
- Ball familiarization (10/30)
- Offense/Team (10/40)
- Goalkeeper warm-up shooting (10/50)
- Offense/Small groups (15/65)
- Offense/Team (15/80)
- Sprint contest (10/90)

Training unit total time: 90 minutes

| TU 1-1 | Warm-up/Stretching | 10 | 10 |

Course:
- The players crisscross the court.
- One player has a ball and decides which move all players should do next (hopping, running backward, jumping with one foot, sit-ups, push-ups...).
- Afterwards he passes the ball to another player who now also may choose a move.

Subsequently, the players perform stretching exercises together; one player chooses an exercise which the other players must do as well.

| TU 1-2 | Coordination run | 10 | 20 |

Basic course:
- Each player should run through the course 3 times in a row with an intensity of 60 to 80%.
- Afterwards, the players may take a short break before they do the course 3 more times in a row, but now with an intensity of 100% during the individual exercises.

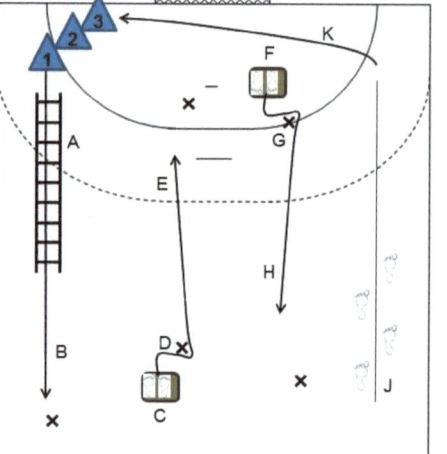

Course:
- ① starts and runs through the coordination ladder with two footsteps per interspace (left and right foot) (A).
- At the end of the coordination ladder, ① sprints to the cone (B).
- ① stands on the small vaulting box with two feet (C), jumps off straight with two feet, dynamically runs to the right and around the cone (D), and finally sprints to the next cone (E).
- Afterwards, the players repeat the course at the next small vaulting box (F, G, and H), but now they should run to the left once they have landed (G).
- ① jumps with one foot (with the left foot in the example) to the left and to the right alternately using a line on the gym floor (1st course with his left foot, 2nd course with his right foot, 3rd course with both feet) (J).
- As soon as he has finished, ① lines up again and repeats the course (K).
- ② starts the same course a bit delayed; and so on.

| TU 1-3 | Ball familiarization | 10 | 30 |

Course:

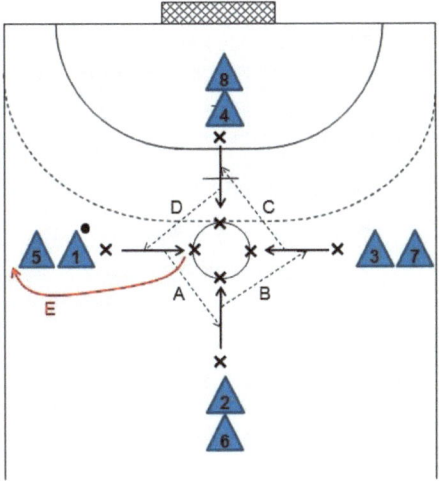

- 1 makes a dynamic piston movement forward and passes the ball to 2, who also makes a piston movement (A); 2 makes a dynamic piston movement forward towards the cone and passes the ball to 3, who also makes a piston movement (B); and so on (C and D).
- After the dynamic piston movement, 1 moves backward diagonally to the right and lines up behind 5 (E); and so on.

Variants:

- 1 and 3 each have a ball and start the course in parallel.
- They pass the ball to the left.

⚠ Make sure the players perform the piston movement in a dynamic manner.

⚠ They should play normal passes; underarm passes are not allowed. The players should rotate their trunk and do a shooting feint when passing the ball.

Special Handball Practice 2 - Step-by-step training of successful offense strategies against the 6-0 defense system

TU 1-4	Offense/Team	10	40

Course:

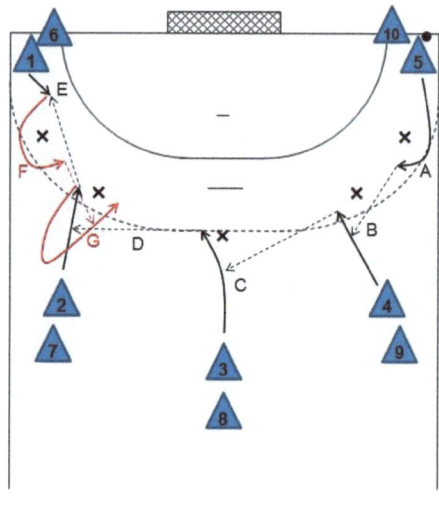

- 5 starts from the wing position and runs a curve around the cone (A), approaches the goal, and passes the ball into the running path of 4 (B).
- 4 does a dynamic piston movement towards the left side of the cone and passes the ball into the running path of 3 (C).
- 3 does a dynamic piston movement towards the left side of the cone and passes the ball into the running path of 2 (D).
- 2 does a dynamic piston movement towards the left side of the cone and passes the ball to 1 on the wing position (E).
- 1 starts from the wing position and runs a curve around the cone (F).
- 2 immediately moves back to the back position after playing the pass (E), does a dynamic piston movement towards the right side of the cone, and receives a pass from 1 into his running path (G).
- Now the players repeat the piston movements towards the right side of the cone until 5 has received the ball again.

Instructions for 2 and 4:
- They both perform two actions: They do a piston movement and pass the ball to 1 (5) on the wing position (E), immediately move back in a dynamic manner, and then do a piston movement towards the other side (G).
- Afterwards, it is the next back position player's turn.

Instructions for 3:
- 3 does two piston movements (coming from the left and coming from the right).
- Afterwards, it is the next center back position player's turn.

Special Handball Practice 2 - Step-by-step training of successful offense strategies against the 6-0 defense system

Instructions for 1 and 5:

- 1 (5) performs two actions; afterwards it is the next player's turn (E and F).

⚠ The players should increase the piston movement and passing speed gradually.

⚠ Make sure the players do the piston movement correctly (towards the left/right side of the cone), depending on the passing/piston movement direction.

TU 1-5	Goalkeeper warm-up shooting	10	50

Course:

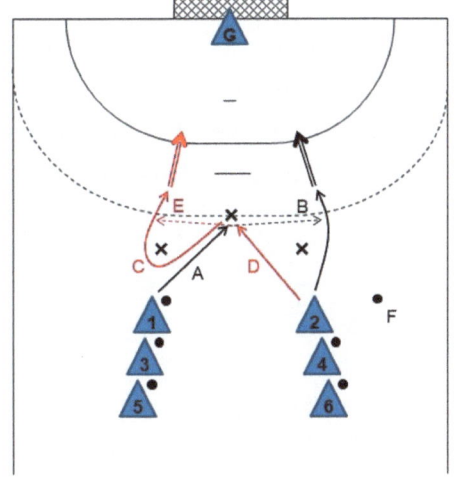

- 1 has a ball and does a dynamic piston movement towards the cone in the center (A).
- 2 does a parallel piston movement towards the right side of the cone, receives a pass from 1 into his running path, and eventually shoots at the right side of the goal, as instructed (top, middle, bottom) (B).
- Immediately after the pass (A), 1 moves back and to the side and runs around the cone (C).
- 4 does a dynamic piston movement towards the cone in the center (D) and passes the ball to 1 into his running path, who eventually shoots at the left side of the goal, as instructed (middle, top, bottom) (E).
- And so on.

⚠ 2 should move back immediately after his shot (B), pick up a new ball (F), and feed the last player.

⚠ The players should do the piston movement towards the cone in the center and the backward move after the pass in a highly dynamic manner.

TU 1-6 — Offense/Small groups — 15 — 65

Course:

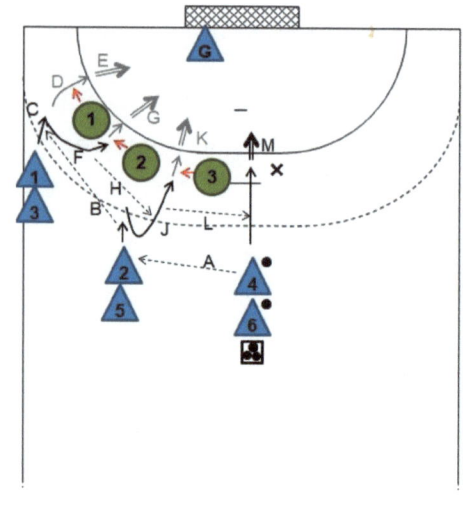

- The players should pass the ball from the center back position to the right/left back position and to the wing position while doing the piston movement (A and B).
- 1 does a piston movement on the wing position (C) and then should decide whether breaking through (D) and shooting from the wing position (E) is an option.
- If there is not enough space on the wing position, 1 dynamically moves towards the gap between 1 and 2 (F), and then decides whether breaking through and shooting is possible (G).
- If 1 cannot break through, he passes the ball (H) to 2 (J) who also does the piston movement.
- 2 must decide whether breaking through and shooting at the goal is an option (K).
- If 2 cannot shoot himself, he passes the ball to 4 (L), who approaches the goal and eventually shoots from the center back position (M).
- Afterwards, the next group of three starts the same course.
- The players line up again, but switch positions.

⚠ The players should approach the goal in a dynamic manner and then decide whether they try to shoot at the goal or not.

⚠ The players should always move towards the gaps (between the defense players).

TU 1-7	Offense/Team		15	80

Description:
- The players should now implement the piston movement they practiced before in a 5-on-5 game.

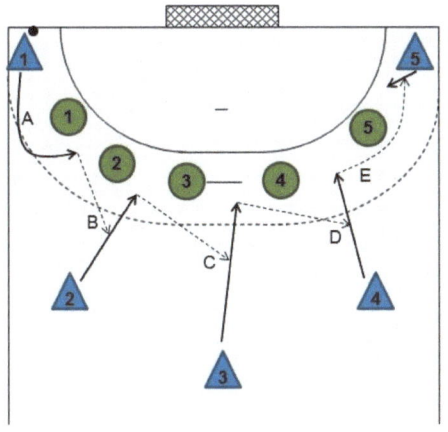

Basic course:
- **Phase 1:** Allow the attacking players to practice the timing of the piston movement and the possible breakthrough for a couple of minutes. Afterwards, change the defense and offense players.
- **Phase 2:** Each team may play 5 attacks. They get a point for each goal. Which team has shot the most goals?

Course:
- 1 does a dynamic piston movement on the wing position (A), moves towards the gap between 1 and 2, and passes the ball into the running path of 2 (B).
- 2 does a piston movement, moving vigorously towards the gap between 2 and 3, and passes the ball into the running path of 3 (C).
- 3 does a piston movement, moving vigorously towards the gap between 3 and 4, and passes the ball into the running path of 4 (D).
- 4 does a piston movement, moving vigorously towards the gap between 4 and 5, and passes the ball to 5 (E) on the wing position.

- If there is enough space for 5 to shoot at the goal, he may shoot. If 5 obstructs the path towards the goal (F), 5 runs a curve, and the players repeat the piston movement while passing the ball to the other side (G, H, J, and K).
- If one of the players is able to break through the defense line during the piston movement, he may shoot at the goal himself.

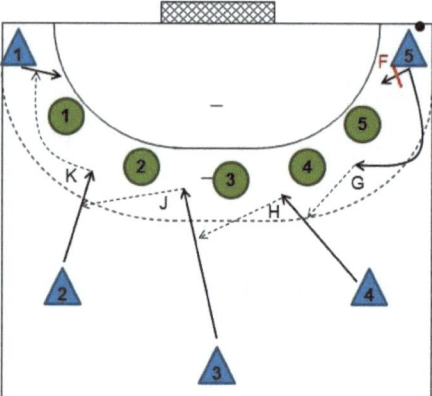

⚠️ The attacking players should seek their own advantage and try to break though themselves before passing the ball to the next player.

⚠️ 1 or 5 should try to shoot at the goal when there is enough space on the outer side of the wing position.

⚠️ The attacking players should move back to their initial position immediately after passing the ball, so that they can approach the goal dynamically during the next piston movement.

| TU 1-8 | Sprint contest | 10 | 90 |

Basic setting:
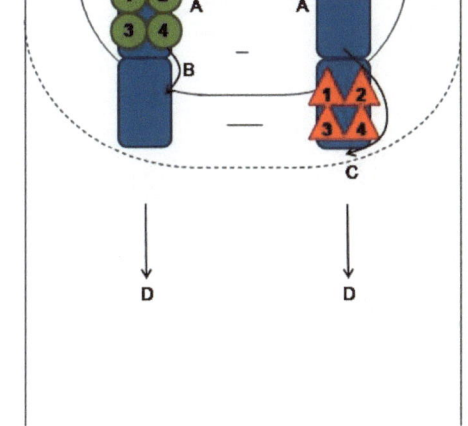
- Make two (or more) teams of four. Each team has two small gym mats.
- The four players all stand on the first mat in the beginning (A).
- They must not touch the gym floor during the competition.
- Define a finish line (e.g. the opposite goal line).

Course:
- The teams start upon command and step onto the second mat (B).
- They now should lift the first mat above their heads and lay it down on the floor in front of the second mat (C).
- The players step onto the mat in the front and repeat the course until they have crossed the finish line (D).

The losing team must do push-ups or sit-ups, for example.

Variant:
- The players may lay the mat on the floor in any way. If a player has touched the ground, his team must go back and start over.

TU 2:		Basics of the crossing movement			★★	90
	Opening part	**Main part**				
X	Warm-up/Stretching		Offense/Individual			Jumping power
	Running exercise		Offense/Small groups		X	Sprint contest
	Short game	X	Offense/Team			Goalkeeper
	Coordination	X	Offense/Series of shots			
	Coordination run		Defense/Individual		**Final part**	
	Strengthening		Defense/Small groups		X	Closing game
X	Ball familiarization		Defense/Team			Final sprint
X	Goalkeeper warm-up shooting		Athletics			
			Endurance			

Key:

  Cone

  Ball box

  Attacking player

  Defense player

Equipment required:
→ 2 ball boxes with sufficient number of handballs, 10 cones

Description:

The objective of this training unit is to develop simple crossing moves. Following warm-up and a coordination run that includes reactions to changing situations, the players develop simple crossing moves during the ball familiarization exercise. In the subsequent goalkeeper warm-up shooting exercise, the crossing moves will be extended by a shot at the goal. Step by step, the players develop a crossing move with a subsequent shot from the back positions until finally, they are able to do two consecutive crossing moves. During the 6-on-6 final game, the players implement what they practiced before.

The training unit consists of the following key exercises:
- Warm-up/Stretching (individual exercise: 10 minutes/total time: 10 minutes)
- Sprint contest (10/20)
- Ball familiarization (10/30)
- Goalkeeper warm-up shooting (10/40)
- Offense/Series of shots (10/50)
- Offense/Series of shots (15/65)
- Offense/Team (15/80)
- Closing game (10/90)

Training unit total time: 90 minutes

Special Handball Practice 2 - Step-by-step training of successful offense strategies against the 6-0 defense system

TU 2-1	Warm-up/Stretching		10	10

Course:
- Four players each crisscross the court together while passing a ball. The passing order always remains the same.
- Upon the coach's whistle, they must change the passing order completely, however. They also must change the pass type (bounce pass, jump shot pass, pass with the non-throwing hand), whereas every player must implement the new pass type (one player of the group defines the new pass type).
- The players perform stretching exercises together.

TU 2-2	Coordination run		10	20

Course 1 (figure 1):
- 1 and 2 start to run simultaneously at relaxed pace once the coach has called out a number (4 in the example).
- 1 and 2 run to the 4th cone on their respective side and touch it lightly (A). Then, both run to the center, exchange high-fives with both hands (B), and run back (C).

Course 2 (figure 2):
- This time, the players need to sprint. The first player who crosses the start line again wins the game. The loser must do an exercise (three push-ups, for example).
- 1 and 2 again start to run simultaneously once the coach has called out a number (24 in the example). The players need to run to the respective cones – hereby, the number of tens applies to the cones on the players' own side (D) and the number of ones to the cones on the opponents' side (E) –, touch them, and run back (F).

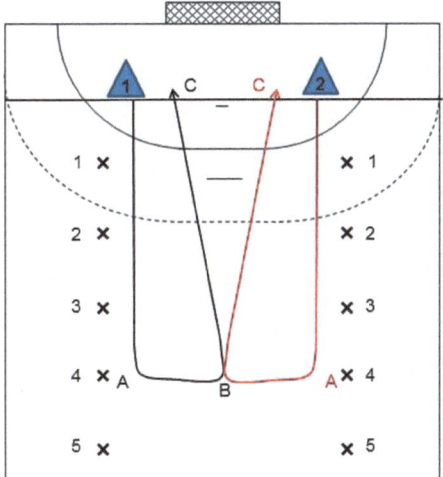

Figure 1

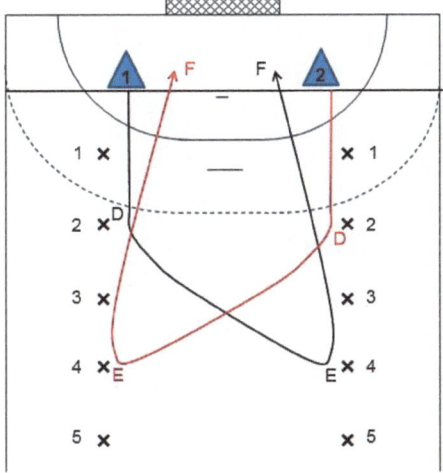

Figure 2

⚠ The coach must call out the numbers loud and clear.

⚠ During course 2, the players should meet in the center so that they need to fight their way through to the next cone, i.e. assert themselves.

| TU 2-3 | Ball familiarization | 10 | 30 |

Course:

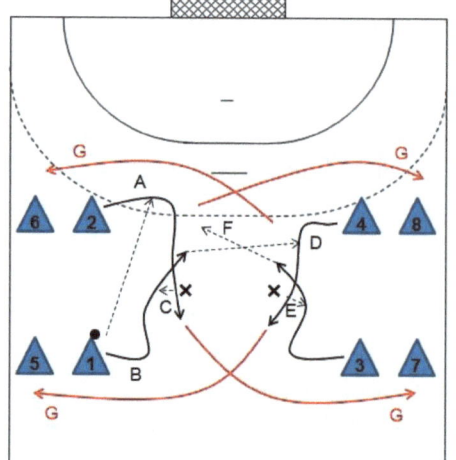

- ② makes a clear running feint to the left, then dynamically runs towards the inner side before receiving a pass from ① into his running path (A).
- ① starts immediately after the pass, runs a few meters straight forward (B), then dynamically runs to the left, takes on the crossing, and finally receives the ball (C).
- ④ runs a few meters straight forward and receives a pass from ① into his running path (D).
- ④ dynamically runs towards the inner side and crosses with ③, who also runs a few meters straight forward before taking on the crossing and receiving the ball (E).
- Afterwards, the players do the same course on the other side, with ③ playing the initial pass to ⑥ (F).
- After the actions, the players line up again on the other side (G).

Variants:
- The players should play the passes after the crossing (D and F) as jump shot passes to the other group.

⚠ The players should initially run straight forward (running feint) in a dynamic manner before starting the crossing move.

| TU 2-4 | Goalkeeper warm-up shooting | 10 | 40 |

Course:

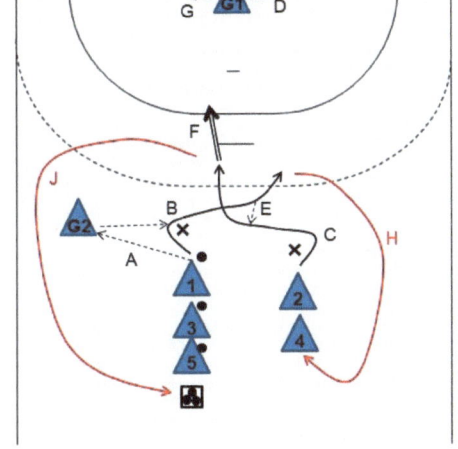

- ① passes the ball to G2 (A), runs around the cone on the left side, and receives a return pass from G2 (B).
- ② makes a running feint towards the right side of the cone, a bit delayed, however (C).
- ①, having the ball, dynamically moves towards the inner side. ② takes on the crossing and receives the ball (E).
- G1 dynamically sidesteps from the center of the goal to the goalpost (D), touches it lightly, and then immediately sidesteps back to the other side. There, he tries to save the ball (G) that is shot by ② at the left side of the goal (F), according to the coach's instruction (top, middle, bottom).

⚠ G1 should time his movements inside the goal in such a way that he can save the shot of ② in motion.

- ③ and ④ start the same course, a bit delayed, however, so that G1 faces a series of shots.
- ① lines up behind the group of shooting players after his action (H); ② picks up a ball and also lines up again (J).

⚠ The players should run around the cones (B and C) and do the transverse crossing move (E) at high speed.

| TU 2-5 | Offense/Series of shots | 10 | 50 |

Course:

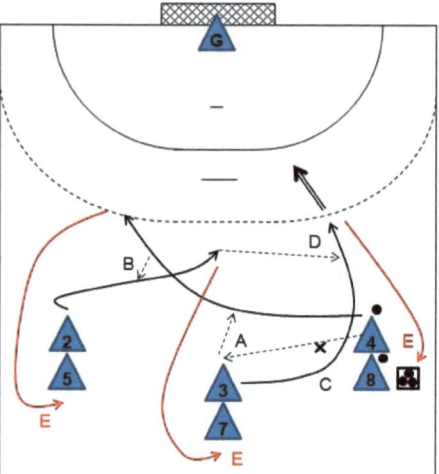

- 4 passes the ball to 3, dynamically runs to the left side, and receives a return pass from 3 into his running path (A).
- 2 makes a running feint to the left side (without a ball) and crosses 4, who plays a pass (B).
- 3 runs around the cone (C) after passing the ball to 4 (A).
- 2 now approaches the goal dynamically and passes the ball to 3 who approaches the goal at full speed (D).
- 3 makes a jump shot at the 9-meter line.
- After the action, the players line up again as shown in the figure (E).
- And so on.

Extension:

- One defense player acts as defensive block against 3.

⚠ 3 must time his start in such a way that he does not have to wait for the pass (D).

Special Handball Practice 2 - Step-by-step training of successful offense strategies against the 6-0 defense system

TU 2-6	Offense/Series of shots	15	65

Course:

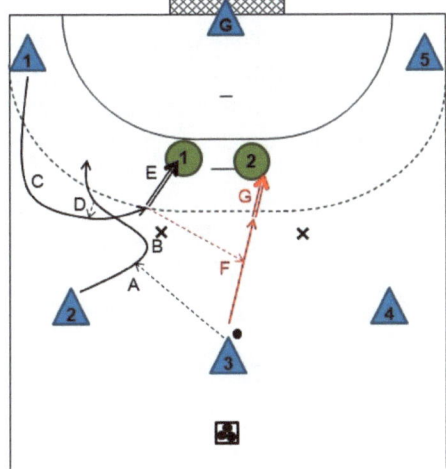

- 3 passes the ball into the running path of 2 towards the center (A) (the cone serves as orientation) (B).
- After the pass, 2 dynamically moves to the wing position. 1 starts from the wing position, runs a curve (C), takes on the crossing of 2, and receives a pass into his running path (D).
- 1 dynamically approaches the goal and makes a jump shot (E). 1 serves as defensive block.
- Afterwards, repeat the course on the other side with 3, 4, and 5, and with 2 being the defense player.
- 1 and 2 switch positions after the action.
- And so on.

Fixed extension:

- 1 passes the ball into the forward running path of 3 after the crossing (F).
- 3 makes a jump shot at the goal. 2 serves as defensive block.

Optional extension:

- 1 determines the further movements of 1, depending on his action:
  o If 1 remains defensive, 1 makes a jump shot at the goal (E).
  o If 1 actively steps forward, the ball should be passed to 3 (F) who then makes a jump shot at the goal (G).

⚠ 1 should always approach the goal vigorously before passing the ball to 3 (F).

Special Handball Practice 2 - Step-by-step training of successful offense strategies against the 6-0 defense system

TU 2-7	Offense/Team		15	80

Course:

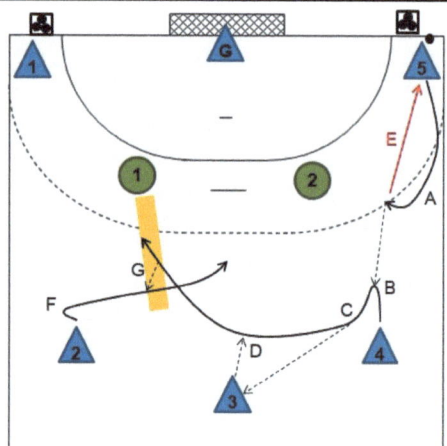

- ⑤ dynamically starts on the wing position, runs a curve, does the piston movement (A), and passes the ball into the running path of ④ (B).
- ④ takes a turn towards the center and immediately passes the ball to ③ (C).
- ④ now runs to the left side at top speed, towards ①, and receives a return pass from ③ into his running path (D).
- ⑤ moves back to the wing position (E) immediately after he played the pass (A).
- ② makes a clear running feint to the left side (without a ball) (F), takes on the crossing of ④, who passes him the ball (G).
- ③ slows down a bit after he passed the ball to ④ (D) and then dynamically runs a curve to the right, before he receives the ball from ② into his running path (H).

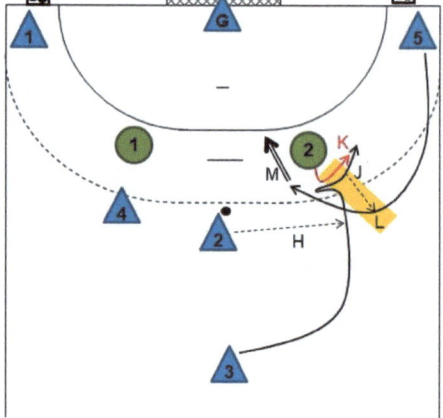

- ③ approaches ② at top speed and must decide as follows:
    o If ② remains defensive, ③ makes a jump shot at the goal, over ②.
    o If ② actively makes a step forward towards ③ (K), ③ plays 1-on-1 against ②, and then forces ② to move along with him towards the wing position (J).
- ⑤ dynamically starts on the wing position, runs a curve, takes on the crossing of ③, receives the ball (L), and makes a jump shot at the goal (M).
- Afterwards, the players repeat the course on the other side; and so on.

⚠️ The players should do the running moves right before and after the crossing (G and L) in a highly dynamic manner.

⚠️ Make sure that the players pass the ball directly at the intersection point, i.e. where the two players cross their paths, so that the defense player cannot see who is holding the ball (colored area).

TU 2-8	Closing game	10	90

Setting:
- Make two teams. Both teams play 6-on-6 against each other.
- Offensive 6-0 defense system with the defense players stepping forward to the 9-meter line vigorously.
- Define an extra task for the losing team beforehand (push-ups, sit-ups, or similar).

Course:
- If a team scores a point as a result of a crossing move (a maximum of 3 passes later), they get two points.

Special Handball Practice 2 - Step-by-step training of successful offense strategies against the 6-0 defense system

TU 3:		Interacting with the pivot		★★	90
Opening part		**Main part**			
X	Warm-up/Stretching		Offense/Individual		Jumping power
	Running exercise	X	Offense/Small groups	X	Sprint contest
X	Short game	X	Offense/Team		Goalkeeper
	Coordination		Offense/Series of shots		
	Coordination run		Defense/Individual	**Final part**	
	Strengthening		Defense/Small groups		Closing game
X	Ball familiarization		Defense/Team		Final sprint
X	Goalkeeper warm-up shooting		Athletics		
			Endurance		

Key:

✗ Cone

🔳 Ball box

🔺1 Attacking player

🟢1 Defense player

⬜ Small vaulting box, upside down

▭ Large vaulting box

Equipment required:
➔ 4 large vaulting boxes, 4 small vaulting boxes, 4 cones per team of 3 sufficient number of handballs

Description:
This training unit focuses on the interaction of the back position players with the pivot. Following a warm-up game and a ball familiarization exercise, the players practice the interaction with the pivot during the goalkeeper warm-up shooting. In the two subsequent exercises, the players further develop and practice the interaction step by step. A sprint contest completes this training unit.

The training unit consists of the following key exercises:
- Warm-up/Stretching (individual exercise: 10 minutes/total time: 10 minutes)
- Short game (10/20)
- Ball familiarization (10/30)
- Goalkeeper warm-up shooting (10/40)
- Offense/Small groups (20/60)
- Offense/Team (20/80)
- Sprint contest (10/90)

Training unit total time: 90 minutes

| TU 3-1 | Warm-up/Stretching | 10 | 10 |

Course:
- Three players each make a team and crisscross the court together while passing a ball.
- The players should always change the running moves (forward, backward, sidestepping).

Variant:
- Two players pass the ball, the third player should try to steal it. While doing this, the two players passing the ball must not dribble, so that they only may do a maximum of three steps before they must play the pass.

The players perform stretching exercises together.

Special Handball Practice 2 - Step-by-step training of successful offense strategies against the 6-0 defense system

| TU 3-2 | Short game | 10 | 20 |

Basic course:
- The players play team ball, without dribbling.
- The teams get a point when they manage to shoot the ball at the outer side of the large vaulting box (i.e. the side facing towards the gym wall).

Course:

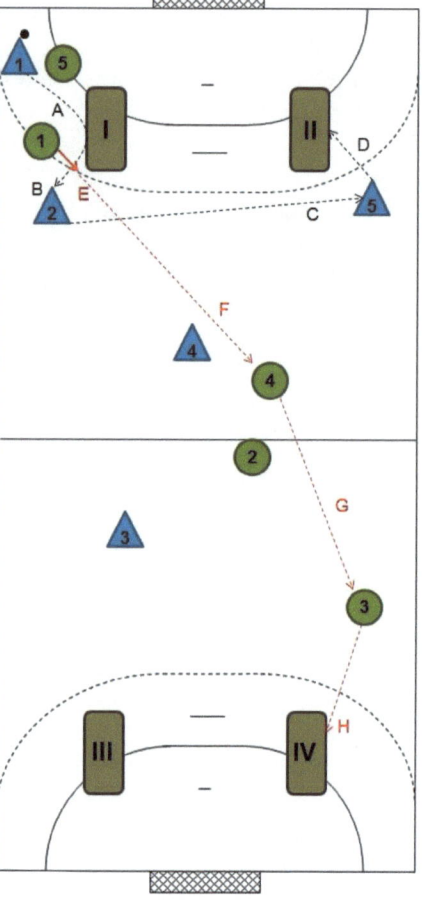

- If ▲1 manages to shoot the ball at the box in such a way (A) that a teammate (here ▲2) can catch it (B), his team may further try to score points. However, the team now has to play on the other box (II) in the same playing field (C and D).
- If the team scores again at box II, they may further try to score points; in this case, the team must play on box I again. And so on.
- If ● 1 steals the ball (E), ● 1, ● 2, ● 3, ● 4, and ● 5 may try to score a point; they must play on the diagonal box (IV), however (i.e. diagonal with regard to the last attempt of 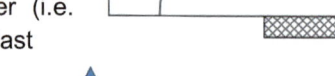 (A)) (F, G, and H).
- If a teammate catches the ball bouncing back from the box (H) 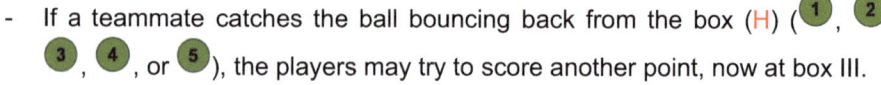), the players may try to score another point, now at box III.

⚠ The player who shot the ball at the box (A and H) is not allowed to catch it again.

Summary of rules:
- If a team steals the ball, they always have to play on the box that stands diagonally to the box at which the other team has tried to score a point least.

| TU 3-3 | Ball familiarization | 10 | 30 |

Basic course:

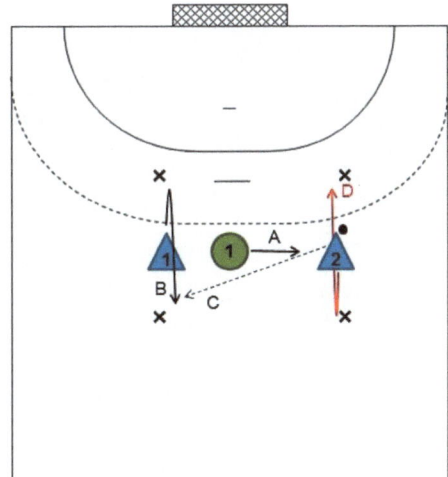

- 1 and 2 must try to pass the ball 10 times, without touching the ball or the player in ball possession.
- The player in ball possession may hold the ball for a maximum of three seconds.
- The players should pass the ball directly or play bounce passes (no banana passes allowed).

Course:

- 1 must approach the player in ball possession (2) actively (A) and try to touch him or to steal the ball (touch it).
- 1 may try to get in a good passing position between the two cones (B); while doing this, he always must stay in line with the cones, however, and must not move to the front or to the back.
- 2 must keep his position with at least one foot after receiving the ball and pass the ball to 1 within three seconds (C), before 1 touches him/it.
- After the pass, 1 touches 2 lightly, before he may try to interrupt the pass from 1 to 2 or to touch 1.
- If 1 touches the ball or the player in ball possession, the players switch positions; they must switch position after 10 passes at the latest, however. If the team manages to play 10 passes, 1 must do 10 quick jumping jacks.

Variant:

- The player in ball possession (here 2) may also move between the two cones during the pass (D).

⚠ 1 should approach the player in ball possession in a highly dynamic manner and try to obstruct the passing path with his arms.

| TU 3-4 | Goalkeeper warm-up shooting | 10 | 40 |

Course:

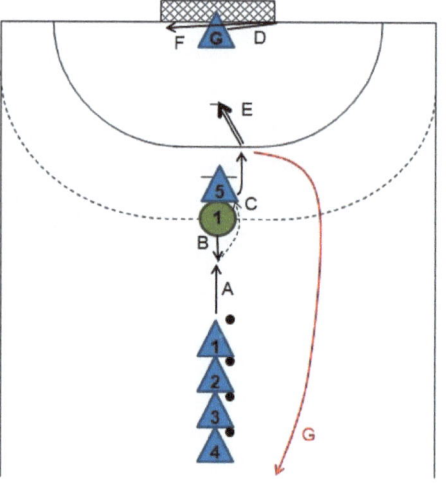

- ▲ dribbles towards ① (A), who steps forward towards him (B) with his arms in the air in order to block the pass.
- ▲ passes the ball to the pivot, around ①, or plays a bounce pass to ▲5 (C). ① should try to make the pass more difficult (C), but allow it.
- Concurrently with the pass (C), G runs to the previously defined starting post (D), touches it lightly, and dynamically moves to the other side in order to save the ball shot by ▲5, as instructed (top, middle, bottom) (E and F).
- ① becomes the new pivot immediately afterwards, ▲ becomes the new defense player. The players repeat the course with ▲2 starting to run. And so on.
- ▲5 sprints to the center line immediately after his shot (G) and lines up again.

⚠ ① should allow the pass (C) to ▲5 and then move backward immediately to become the new pivot. ▲ should also adjust to his new task as a defense player immediately after playing the pass (C).

TU 3-5	Offense/Small groups		20	60

Basic course (figure 1):

- 3 passes the ball to 2 (A).
- 2 does a dynamic piston movement to the left and passes the ball back to 3, who also does a dynamic piston movement to the left (B).
- 3 now dynamically dribbles towards the inner side (C).
- 6 makes a step in the opposite direction and places a screen on the inner side, next to 1 (D).
- 2 makes a step forward towards 3 (E) and 3 passes the ball to 6 (F) who eventually shoots at the goal (G).

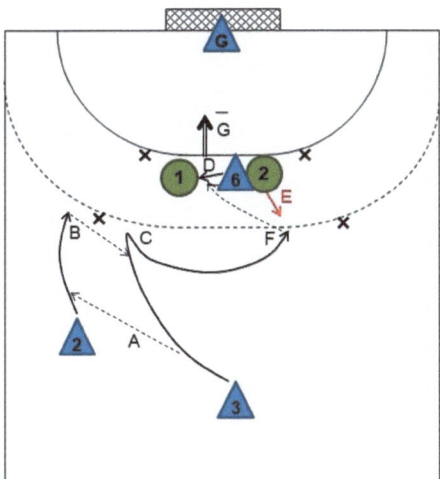

Figure 1

1st extension (figure 2):

- The players start as before (A, B, C, and D).
- 2 should now stay in the back as defensive block so that 3 shoots at the right side of the goal once he has clearly moved to the right (H).

⚠ By clearly moving to the right side, next to 2, the long corner is probably unattended; 3 should take advantage of this situation and shoot accordingly (J).

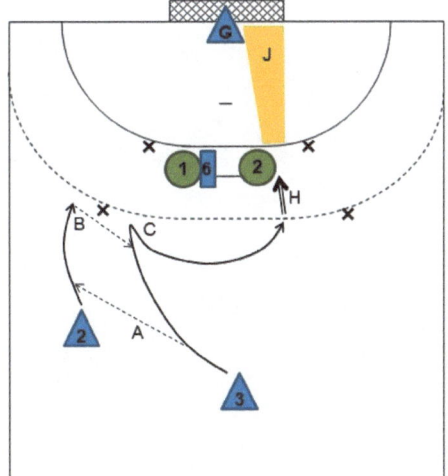

Figure 2

2nd extension (figure 3):

- The players start as before (A, B, C, and D).
- ② now vigorously steps forward towards ▲3 again who tries to get past ② 1-on1 (K and M).
- If his breakthrough attempt fails, ▲3 should try to pass the ball to ▲6 (L).

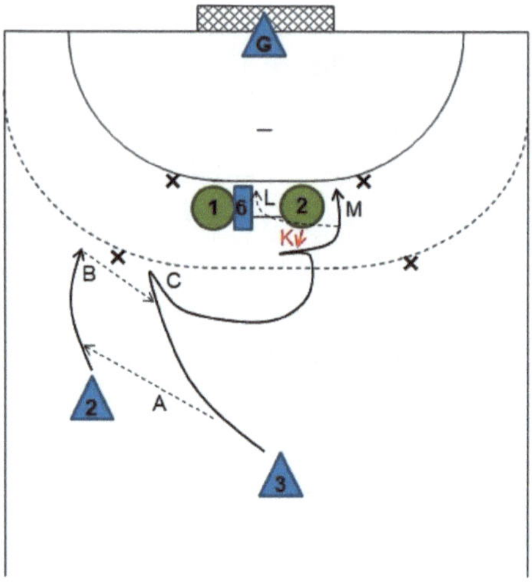

3nd extension:

- ② should now act variably so that ▲3 must choose the right option of the three variants practiced before.

Figure 3

⚠ ② and ▲3 should try to shift the game to the left side already in the beginning (A and B).

⚠ ▲6 must find the right timing for his screen, i.e. he should move in the opposite direction as soon as ▲3 moves (C) to ① (D).

⚠ ▲6 should keep the screening position for a long time and move last minute, i.e. only after ▲3 has played the pass.

TU 3-6	Offense/Team		20	80

Initial action (figure 1):

- ④ passes the ball into the running path of ③ (A).
- ③ immediately passes the ball to ② (B).
- ② does a dynamic piston movement to the left and passes the ball back to ③ (C), who also does a dynamic piston movement to the left (D).
- ③ now dynamically dribbles towards the inner side (E).
- ⑥ makes a step in the opposite direction and places a screen on the inner side, next to ③ (F).

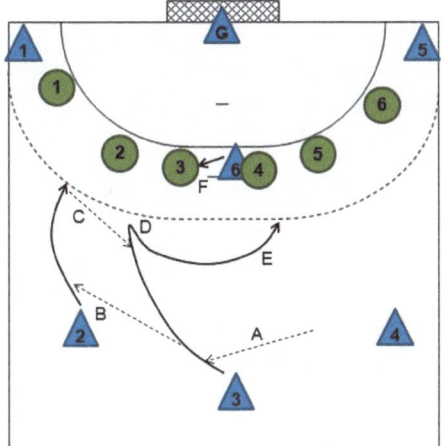

Figure 1

Continuous playing (figure 2):

Depending on the defense players' behavior, ③ should decide as follows:

- If ④ remains defensive and oriented towards ⑥, ③ should move to the right, approach the gap next to ④, and shoot at the goal (J).

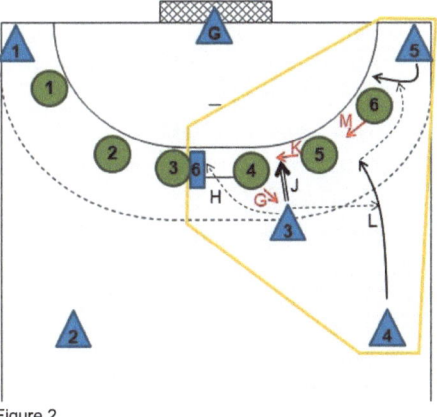

Figure 2

- If ④ vigorously steps forward (G), ③ either may try to pass the ball to ⑥ directly (H) or to initially play 1-on-1 against ④ and break through, or pass the ball to ⑥.
- If ⑤ moves to the inner side (K), in order to support his teammate (i.e. passing the ball to ⑥ is not possible), ③ passes the ball into the running path of ④ who dynamically approaches the gap between ⑤ and ⑥ (L).
- If ⑥ (M) supports his teammates at the inner side, ④ may either break through or pass the ball to ⑤ who eventually shoots at the goal.

⚠️ The players should do the piston and running movements in a dynamic and authentic manner so that the defense players must react accordingly. If a breakthrough is possible or if ▲6 is in a good position for a pass, the players should make use of the advantage.

Objective of the initial action:
- As a result of the movements of ▲2 and ▲3 along with the screening of ▲6, the players should be able to pass the ball to ▲6 or to create an outnumbered situation on the right side (see highlighted section in figure 2).

Competition:
- Each team plays 5 attacks and gets a point for each goal. Which team scores highest?

TU 3-7	Final sprint	10	90

Setting:
- Each team gets a ball box and two cones to define the starting line.
- Position one small vaulting box each on the other side of the playing field.
- Define the running path with a cone.

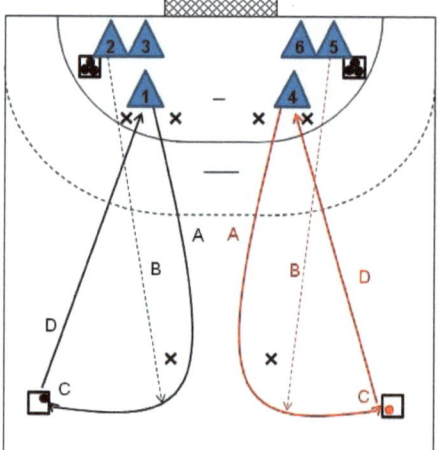

Course:
- ▲1 and ▲4 sprint around the cone (A).
- As soon as they have arrived the cone, they receive a pass from ▲2 or ▲5 (B), and finally put the ball into the box (C).
- Afterwards, they sprint back to their team (D) and exchange a high-five with the next player (▲2 or ▲5).
- Which team has carried all the balls from one box to the other fastest?
- The losing team must do a previously defined penalty exercise.

⚠️ Adjust the passing distance to the players' level of performance by positioning the cones accordingly.

⚠️ Each player should first pass a ball and then make a sprint.

⚠️ The first player passes the ball to the last player.

Special Handball Practice 2 - Step-by-step training of successful offense strategies against the 6-0 defense system

TU 4:	Long crossing of the center back and the wing player as initial action – Part 1		★★★	90

Opening part		Main part			
X	Warm-up/Stretching		Offense/Individual		Jumping power
	Running exercise		Offense/Small groups		Sprint contest
X	Short game	X	Offense/Team		Goalkeeper
	Coordination		Offense/Series of shots		
	Coordination run		Defense/Individual		**Final part**
	Strengthening		Defense/Small groups	X	Closing game
X	Ball familiarization		Defense/Team		Final sprint
X	Goalkeeper warm-up shooting		Athletics		
			Endurance		

Key:

✗ Cone

▦ Ball box

▲ Attacking player

● Defense player

○ Hoop

☐ Small vaulting box, upside down

Equipment required:
→ 6 cones, 6 hoops, 4 small vaulting boxes (upside down), 2 ball boxes with sufficient number of handballs

Description:
This training unit focuses on the development of a simple initial action with crossing of the center back and the wing player. Following a short warm-up game, the players gradually develop the initial action during the ball familiarization phase. After the goalkeeper warm-up shooting, there are two team exercises during which the players practice the running moves of the initial action as well as several options for continued playing and variants. A closing game completes this training unit.

The training unit consists of the following key exercises:
- Warm-up/Stretching (individual exercise: 15 minutes/total time: 15 minutes)
- Short game (10/25)
- Ball familiarization (15/40)
- Goalkeeper warm-up shooting (10/50)
- Offense/Team (15/65)
- Offense/Team (15/80)
- Closing game (10/90)

Training unit total time: 90 minutes

Special Handball Practice 2 - Step-by-step training of successful offense strategies against the 6-0 defense system

| TU 4-1 | Warm-up/Stretching | 15 | 15 |

Course:
- Two players each crisscross the court and easily pass a handball back and forth (short and long passes).
- At the same time, they try to steal the ball from another group. However, they have to keep passing their own ball. If they win another ball, they have to play passes with two balls at a time.

The players perform stretching exercises together.

| TU 4-2 | Short game | 10 | 25 |

Setting:
- Make two teams.
- Position a small vaulting box upside down in each corner of the playing field.
- Put some hoops on the gym floor as well.

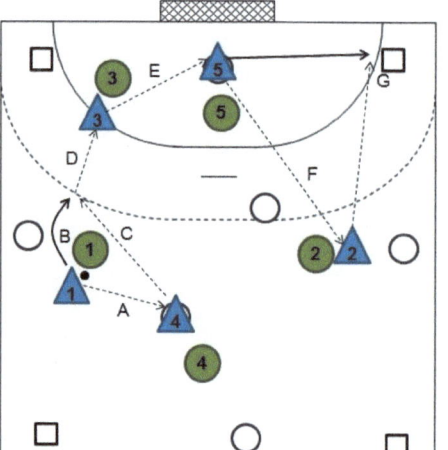

Course:
- By playing quick passes and moving in a well-coordinated manner, the team in ball possession tries to score a point as follows:
    o They initially pass the ball twice to one of their teammates who stands inside a hoop (A, E) and who passes the ball back (C) or to another teammate (F). (While doing this, they must use two different hoops.)
    o Afterwards, they must put the ball into one of the boxes (G).
- The players may play any number of passes in between the passes to the player inside the hoop (D), and also before they put the ball in the box.
- If, in the meantime, the opposing team wins the ball, they must start with passing the ball to a player inside a hoop again.
- Which team scores highest?

⚠ If a player inside a hoop receives the ball, the other players must immediately try to get into a good passing position so that the player in the hoop may play a return pass to one of his teammates (B).

⚠ As soon as the players have passed the ball to teammates inside the hoop twice, they must adjust immediately and play on the small vaulting boxes.

TU 4-3	Ball familiarization		15	40

Course:

- 6 starts the course by passing the ball to 2 (A).
- 2 passes the ball into the running path of 3 (B), who dynamically moves to the right.
- 5 starts on the wing position, takes on the crossing, and receives a pass from 3 (C).
- 4 runs to the left and receives the ball from 5, who dynamically runs to the center (D).
- 4 passes the ball to 1, who runs a curve and passes the ball to 6 again (E).
- Afterwards, 6 passes the ball to 8, and the players repeat the course on the other side.
- And so on.

Positions after the first round:

- 1 and 5 immediately move back to the wing positions dynamically, i.e. they keep their positions.
- 3 and 4 switch positions.
- 6 keeps his position at the 6-meter line.

| TU 4-4 | Goalkeeper warm-up shooting | 10 | 50 |

Course:

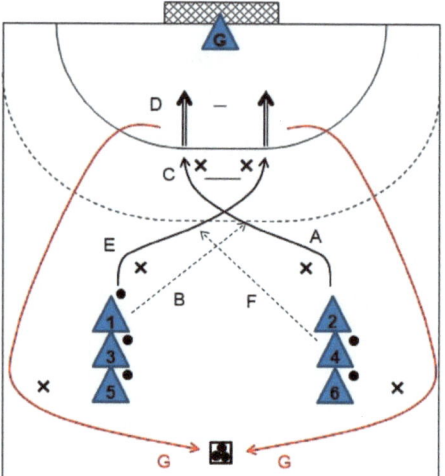

- 2 starts by running around the cone and then diagonally to the left (A).
- 1 passes the ball into the running path of 2 (B).
- 2 runs around the cone and shoots at the goal from within the corridor (C and D).
- 1 also runs around the cone and then diagonally to the right (E), once he has passed the ball to 2 (B).
- 4 passes the ball into the running path of 1 (F), and 1 finally shoots at the goal.
- After the shot, the shooting players make a sprint to the ball box and line up again (G).
- The players repeat the course until there is no ball left in the box.

TU 4-5	Offense/Team		15	65

Course:

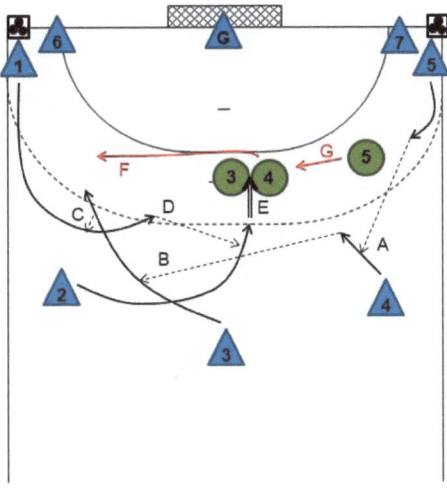

- 5 does a piston movement with a ball and passes it into the piston movement path of 4 (A).
- 5 tries to interrupt the piston movement of 5 and the pass to 4.
- 3 dynamically runs to the left and receives a pass from 4 into his piston movement path (B).
- 1 dynamically runs a curve, takes on the crossing of 3, and receives a pass (C).
- 1 approaches the goal and passes the ball into the running path of 2, who dynamically runs a long curve (D).
- 2 makes a jump shot over the defensive block of 3 and 4 (E).
- Afterwards, the players start the course over with 1 starting the piston movement on the other side.
- And so on.

Repositioning after the course:

- 1 moves back to his initial wing position.
- 2 and 3 switch positions and move to their new positions immediately after the action.
- The defense players move to the left side (F and G).

TU 4-6	Offense/Team		15	80

Course:

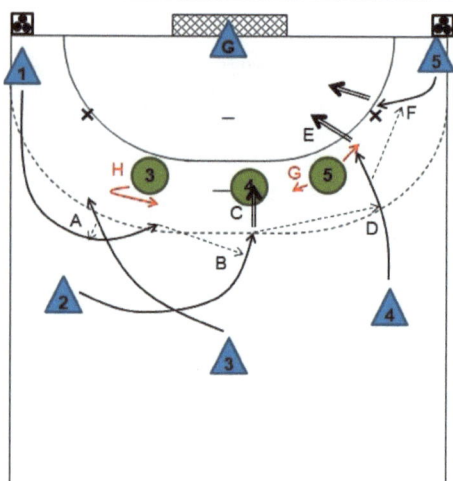

- The players start the piston movement on the right side (not shown in the figure).
- 3 receives the ball from 4 into his running path, does a dynamic piston movement to the left, and crosses with 1, who dynamically starts from the wing position and runs a curve (A).
- 1 approaches the goal and passes the ball into the running path of 2 who dynamically runs a long curve (B).
- 2 must decide now:
    o If 4 remains defensive and keeps his position, 2 makes a jump shot at the goal (C).
    o If 4 makes a step forward, 2 dynamically does a piston movement towards the goal and passes the ball into the running path of 4 (D).
- 4 must decide now:
    o If 5 is oriented towards the center (G), 4 breaks through dynamically and eventually shoots at the goal (E).
    o If 5 moves along towards the back position, 4 does a piston movement towards the goal and plays a bounce pass to 5 on the wing position, who eventually shoots at the goal (F).
- Afterwards, the players do the same course on the other side.
- And so on.

⚠ 3 should interrupt the movements of 3 and 1 more and more vigorously during the course of the exercise (H).

⚠ The players should do the piston movement towards the goal in a vigorous and dynamic manner.

⚠ The players should always try to score a goal themselves (2 and 4).

| TU 4-7 | Closing game | 10 | 90 |

Basic setting:
- Make two teams. Both teams play handball against each other.
- Defense system: 6-0.

Course:
- If a team scores a goal by implementing what they practiced before, they get an extra point.
- Define an extra exercise for the losing team before the game.

Afterwards, the players jog a few minutes and perform stretching exercises together.

TU 5:	Long crossing of the center back and the wing player as initial action – Part 2			★★★	90
	Opening part		**Main part**		
X	Warm-up/Stretching		Offense/Individual		Jumping power
	Running exercise		Offense/Small groups	X	Sprint contest
X	Short game	X	Offense/Team		Goalkeeper
	Coordination		Offense/Series of shots		
	Coordination run		Defense/Individual		**Final part**
	Strengthening		Defense/Small groups	X	Closing game
X	Ball familiarization		Defense/Team		Final sprint
X	Goalkeeper warm-up shooting		Athletics		
			Endurance		

Key:

 Attacking player

 Defense player

 Small gym mat

 Ball box

Equipment required:
➔ 4 small gym mats, 2 ball boxes with sufficient number of handballs

Description:
In this training unit, the players gradually further develop the initial action of the previous training unit and practice further possible solutions. Following a short warm-up game, the players develop the running paths during the ball familiarization phase. The goalkeeper warm-up shooting includes a simple crossing move with a subsequent shot at the goal. During two team exercises, the players practice the different playing options that are to be implemented in the subsequent closing game.

The training unit consists of the following key exercises:
- Warm-up/Stretching (individual exercise: 15 minutes/total time: 15 minutes)
- Short game (10/25)
- Ball familiarization (10/35)
- Goalkeeper warm-up shooting (10/45)
- Offense/Team (15/60)
- Offense/Team (20/80)
- Closing game (10/90)

Training unit total time: 90 minutes

TU 5-1	Warm-up/Stretching	15	15

Course:
The players independently warm-up, each with a ball. If two players "meet", they do the following:
- Exchange a high five with one hand.
- Shortly touch each other with the foot.
- Jump into the air and exchange a high five there.
- Jump into the air and bump into each other at chest level.
- Exchange handballs.

The players perform stretching exercises together.

TU 5-2	Short game	10	25

Setting:
- Position 4 small gym mats in the corners of the playing field (in such a way that the players can step onto them on each side).

Course:
- By passing quickly (A and B) and moving in a well-coordinated manner, the attacking team tries to score a point.
- They score a point when they manage to pass the ball to a player (C) who sits on the back of a teammate on a mat (piggyback).
- A team may score several points in a row, but not on the same mat, however.
- The other team tries to steal the ball and score points themselves. They must not step on the mats.

Variant:
- The players only score a point, if the player on the mat (sitting on his teammates' back) (C) receives a pass and passes the ball to another teammate (D).

⚠ The players must run in a well-coordinated manner and work as a team in order to give each other the piggyback and score a point.

TU 5-3 — Ball familiarization — 10 — 35

Course (figure 1):

- 6 starts the course by passing the ball to 2 (A).
- 2 passes the ball into the running path of 3, who dynamically moves to the right (B).
- 5 starts on the wing position, takes on the crossing, and receives a pass from 3 (C).
- 4 runs to the left and receives the ball from 5, who dynamically runs to the center (D).
- 4 passes the ball to 1, who runs a curve and passes the ball to 6 again (E).
- Afterwards, 6 passes the ball to 8, and the players repeat the course on the other side.

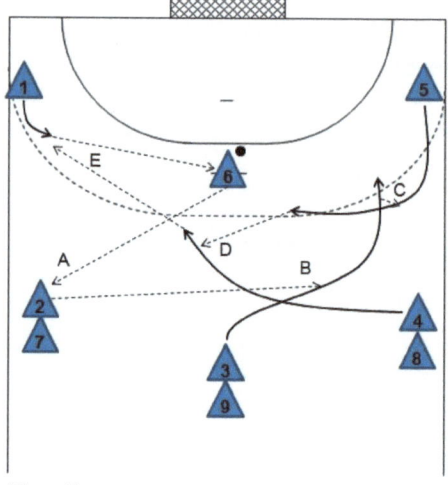

(Figure 1)

Positions after the first round:

- 1 and 5 immediately move back to the wing positions dynamically, i.e. they keep their positions.
- 3 and 4 switch positions after the crossing.
- 6 keeps his position at the 6-meter line.

Extension (figures 2 and 3):

- The initial passes (A, B, C, and D) remain the same.
- After the crossing of ▲3 and ▲5, both players move back again – ▲3 to the left wing position and ▲5 to the right back position (see figure 3).
- ▲4 dynamically moves far to the left, crosses with ▲2, and passes him the ball (F).
- ▲5 dynamically does a piston movement while receiving the pass from ▲2 into his running path (G).
- ▲3 runs a curve, receives a pass from ▲5 into his running path (H), and passes the ball to ▲6 again (J).
- Afterwards, ▲6 passes the ball to ▲8, and the players repeat the course on the other side.

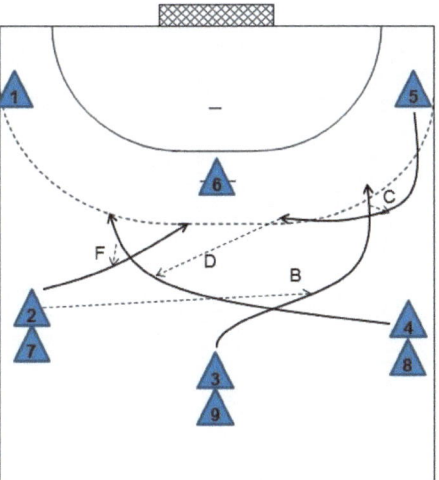

(Figure 2)

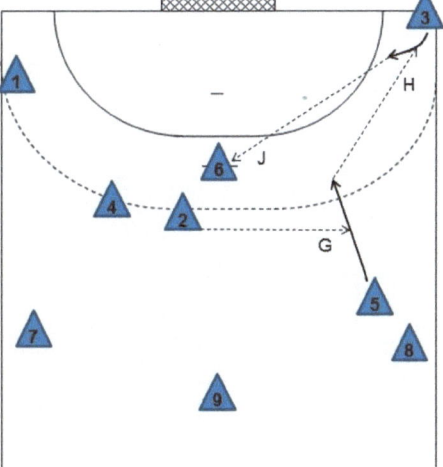

(Figure 3)

| TU 5-4 | Goalkeeper warm-up shooting | 10 | 45 |

Course:

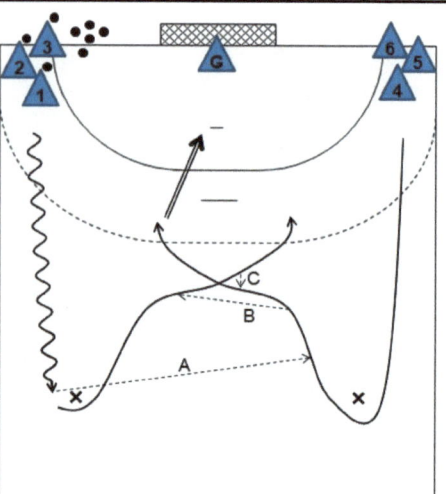

- 1 and 4 start simultaneously, while 1 is dribbling the ball.
- Both run around the cone.
- Immediately after they have surrounded the cone, 1 passes the ball (A) to 4.
- Immediate return pass (B) to 1, who immediately starts a crossing move.
- 4 crosses behind him and receives a pass from 1 (C).
- The players shoot alternately, as instructed (top, middle, bottom).
- The second group should start a bit delayed, so that there is a smooth rhythm for the goalkeeper.

Variants:
- Jump shot.
- Shooting with the wrong foot in front.
- Jump shot pass (drop the ball in the air on the back side during the crossing).
- Balls on the other side -> The players do the same course inversely.

TU 5-5	Offense/Team		15	60

Course:

- 5 starts the piston movement on the wing position and passes the ball into the running path of 4 (A).
- 3 makes a clear running feint to the right side (B), receives a pass from 4 into his running path (C), and then moves to the left.
- 1 starts from the wing position, runs a curve, takes on the crossing, and receives a pass (D).
- 1 approaches the goal and passes the ball into the running path of 2, who dynamically runs a long curve to the right (E).
- 3 runs to the wing position immediately after the pass (H), and 1 runs to the left back position (J).
- 4 initially runs along in parallel within the corridor (F), but then takes on the crossing, and receives a pass (G).
- 4 does a dynamic piston movement towards the goal and passes the ball into the running path of 1 (K).
- 1 does a dynamic piston movement towards the goal and plays a bounce pass to 3 (L), who eventually shoots at the goal (M).
- Afterwards, the players repeat the course on the other side.
- And so on.
- The defense players should make a step forward towards the attacking players and try to interrupt the pass, if an attacking player holds the ball for too long.

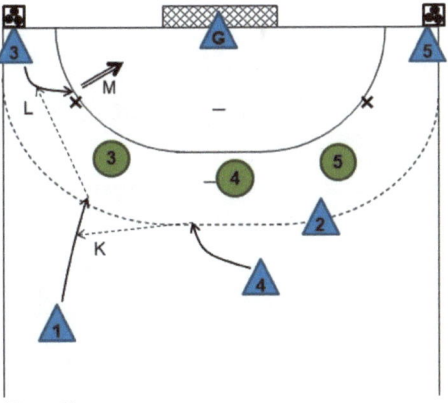

(Figure 1)

(Figure 2)

⚠ After the parallel piston movement of 4 (F), the players should speed up considerably and pass the ball in a highly dynamic and speedy manner!

TU 5-6	Offense/Team		20	80

Basic setting:
- 5-on-5 play.
- The attacking players and the defense players switch tasks after each attack.
- For each goal the players score by implementing the following, they get a point. Who has scored 3 (5) points first?

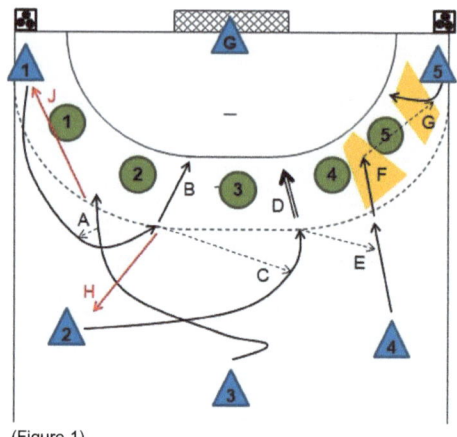

(Figure 1)

Course:

- 5 starts the piston movement on the wing position and passes the ball into the running path of 4 (as in the exercises before; not shown in the figure), and moves to the left.

- 4 now should observe the defense players before the next action: If the defense players move together, 4 does a straight forward piston movement:
    o If the gap between 4 and 5 remains open, he shoots at the goal himself (F).
    o If the defense players close the gap, he plays a bounce pass to 5, and 5 shoots at the goal from the wing position (G).

- 4 now should observe the defense players before the next action: If the defense players move together, 4 does a straight forward piston movement:
    o If the gap between 4 and 5 remains open, he shoots at the goal himself (F).
    o If the defense players close the gap, he plays a bounce pass to 5, and 5 shoots at the goal from the wing position (G).

Alternative continuous playing option:

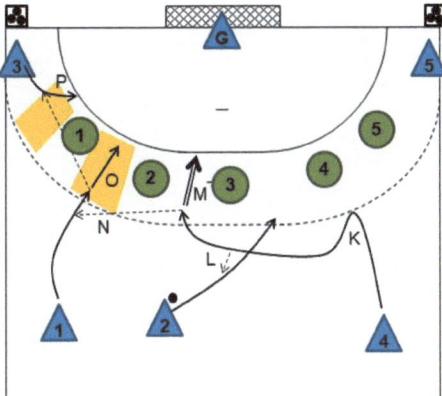

- If the defense players (4 and 5) stand in a correct position and do not stand close enough to each other, 4 stops his position movement (K), makes a counter piston movement, takes on the crossing of 2, and receives the ball (L).
- 4 must vigorously approach the gap between 2 and 3, try to break through, and shoot at the goal (M).

(Figure 2)

- If 4 cannot break through (M), 4 passes the ball to 1 into his dynamic piston movement (N) towards the gap between 1 and 2.
- 1 tries to break through in a highly dynamic manner (O). If he does not succeed, 1 passes the ball into the running path of 3 on the wing position, and 3 eventually shoots at the goal (P).
- Afterwards, the players repeat the course on the other side.

TU 5-7	Closing game	10	90

Basic setting:
- Make two teams. Both teams play handball against each other.

Course:
- Both teams must start with the initial action they practiced before (either on the left or on the right side). Afterwards, they may play freely (depending on the game situation).
- If a team scores a point as a direct result of the initial action they practiced before, they get **ONE** additional attack starting from the center line.

Afterwards, the players jog a few minutes together.

TU 6:	Focus: Long crossing of the center back and the wing player as initial action – Part 3		★★★	90
Opening part		**Main part**		
X	Warm-up/Stretching		Offense/Individual		Jumping power
	Running exercise		Offense/Small groups	X	Sprint contest
	Short game	X	Offense/Team		Goalkeeper
	Coordination	X	Offense/Series of shots		
X	Coordination run		Defense/Individual	**Final part**	
	Strengthening		Defense/Small groups		Closing game
X	Ball familiarization		Defense/Team		Final sprint
X	Goalkeeper warm-up shooting		Athletics		
			Endurance		

Key:

✕   Cone

▦   Ball box

▲   Attacking player

●   Defense player

▯   Hurdle

▭   Coordination ladder

▬   Small gym mat

Equipment required:
- ➔ 1 coordination ladder, 2 hurdles, 9 cones, 1 small gym mat, 1 ball box with sufficient number of handballs

Description:

In this training unit, the players take up the initial action of the two previous training units and practice further possible solutions. Following warm-up with a coordination run, the players develop an additional crossing move during the ball familiarization exercise and the goalkeeper warm-up shooting. The players further develop this step by step in a series of shots. In a team exercise, the players combine the new crossing move with the initial action they practiced before and eventually implement both in a 6-on-6 game. A sprint contest completes this training unit.

The training unit consists of the following key exercises:
- Warm-up/Stretching (individual exercise: 10 minutes/total time: 10 minutes)
- Coordination run (10/20)
- Ball familiarization (10/30)
- Goalkeeper warm-up shooting (10/40)
- Offense/Series of shots (25/65)
- Offense/Team (20/85)
- Sprint contest (5/90)

Total training time: 90 minutes

Special Handball Practice 2 - Step-by-step training of successful offense strategies against the 6-0 defense system

| TU 6-1 | Warm-up/Stretching | 10 | 10 |

Course 1:
- The players make pairs.
- One player runs in the front and does various running moves (forward, sidestep, hopping, arm rotation, jumping, and so on).
- His teammate runs 1 to 2 meters behind and does the same moves.
- Upon the coach's whistle, the players switch tasks.

Course 2:
- The players make pairs again.
- The two players stand face-to-face at a distance of 1 to 2 meters.
- One player defines the running direction (forward, sidestep, backward) and the running speed.
- The other player should react accordingly and do the same running moves. While doing this, the players should keep the same distance and make sure that both keep moving face-to-face (feet in stepping position).

The players perform stretching exercises together.

| TU 6-2 | Coordination run | 10 | 20 |

Course:

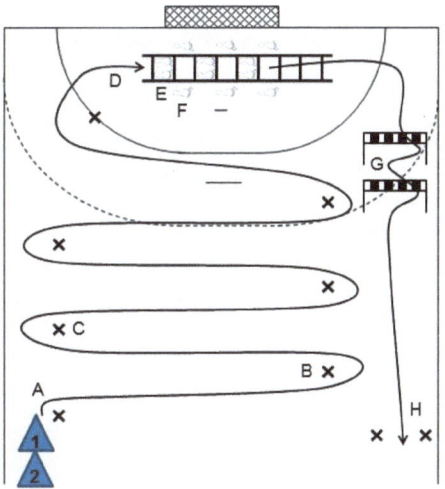

- 1 starts, runs around the first cone (A), sprints to the next cone at high speed (B), runs around it, sprints to the next cone (C), and so on, until he has arrived the last cone.
- 1 does jumping jacks through the coordination ladder (D). While doing this, he should alternately land as follows: with both feet in the interspace (E), with one foot on the left and one foot on the right side of the coordination ladder (F). He should go on until he has arrived at the end of the ladder.
- Afterwards, 1 runs to the two hurdles, jumps over them with both feet (G), and finally sprints through the cone goal (H).
- The other players start the same course a bit delayed.

Basic course:
- The players should do the first two rounds with an intensity of about 70%; afterwards, they may take a short break.
- The players should do the subsequent two rounds with an intensity of 100%.

| TU 6-3 | Ball familiarization | 10 | 30 |

Course:

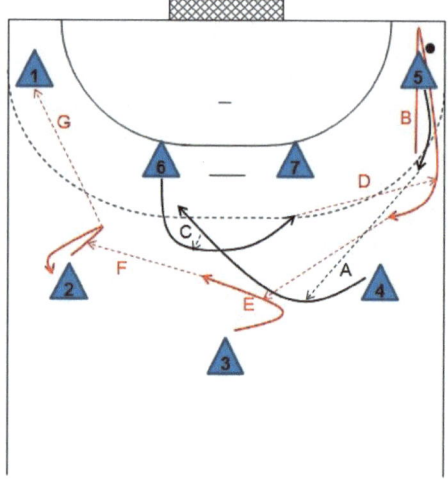

- 5 does a dynamic piston movement (A) and passes the ball to 4 who is running towards the center (A).
- 5 moves back to the wing position immediately after playing the pass (B).
- 4 has the ball and runs far to the left, next to the 7-meter line.
- 6 starts at the 6-meter line and runs a curve, takes on the crossing of 4 (C), and passes the ball into the running path of 5 (D), who has started running from the wing position.
- 3 runs to the right towards 5 and receives a pass from 5 (E).
- 3 does a piston movement to the left and passes the ball into the piston movement path of 2 (F).
- 2 passes the ball to 1 on the wing position (G).
- Afterwards, the players repeat the course on the other side with 2 and 7 doing the crossing movement.
- And so on.

| TU 6-4 | Goalkeeper warm-up shooting | 10 | 40 |

Course:

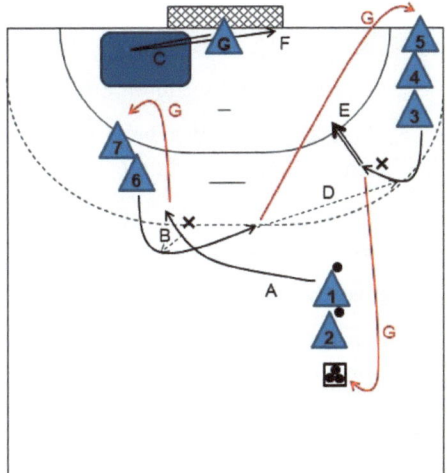

- 1 has a ball and runs far to the left, next to the 7-meter line (A).
- 6 starts at the 6-meter line and runs a curve, takes on the crossing of 1 (B), and passes the ball into the running path of 3 (D), who has started running from the wing position.
- G starts from the center and runs to the small gym mat, where he does a somersault (C).
- 3 runs around the cone and shoots at the right side of the goal, as instructed (top, middle, bottom) (E).
- G moves back to the goal dynamically after the somersault (C) and tries to save (F) the ball shot by 3 (E).
- Following the action, 1, 3, and 6 line up at the next position (G), and the players repeat the course. And so on.
- Change sides after a while.

⚠️ G should time his action (C and F) in such a way that he is able to perform a smooth motion.

TU 6-5	Offense/Series of shots	25	65

Course:

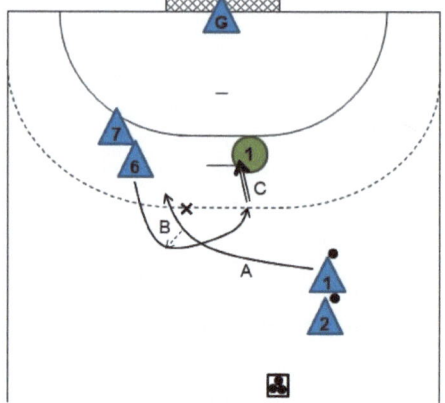

- 1 has a ball and runs far to the left, next to the 7-meter line (A).
- 6 starts from the pivot position, runs a curve, takes on the crossing of 1 (B), and makes a jump shot at the goal, over the block of 1 (C).
- Repeat the course with 2 and 7; and so on.

Extension 1:

- 1 steps forward towards the movement path of 6 (D).
- 2 starts and runs a curve, receives the ball from 6 into his running path (E), and makes a jump shot at the goal (F).

Extension 2:

- 1 and 2 make a step forward towards the movement path of 6 (D) and 2 (G).
- 5 starts from the wing position, receives the ball from 2 into his running path (H), and shoots at the goal from the wing position (J).

Team play:

- 1 and 2 should behave variably in the defense (blocking defensively or actively stepping forward towards the attacking player (D and G)).
- 6 and 2 should react to the movements of 1 and 2 and either shoot over the defensive block (C and F) or keep passing the ball to 5 on the wing position (H).

TU 6-6	Offense/Team		20	85

Course:

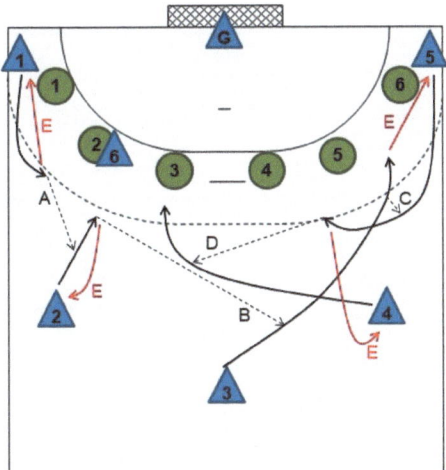

- 1 dynamically starts the piston movement on the wing position and passes the ball into the piston movement path of 2 (A).
- 2 does a dynamic piston movement towards the goal and passes the ball to the right, into the running path of 3 (B).
- 3 does a dynamic piston movement to the right, towards the gap between 5 and 6.
- 5 starts from the wing position, runs a curve, takes on the crossing of 3, and receives a pass (C).
- 5 approaches the goal while holding the ball and plays a pass into the running path of 4 who dynamically runs far to the left, next to the 7-meter line (D).
- Following the first actions, the players immediately move back to their positions, as shown in the figure (E).

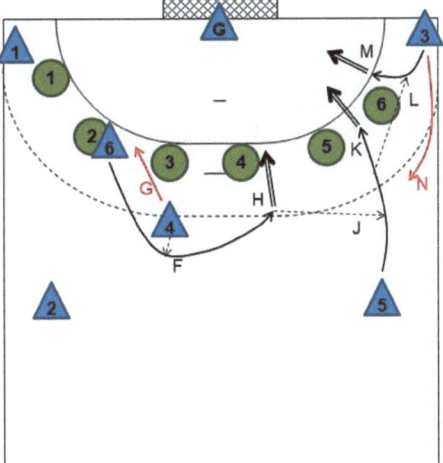

- 6 starts from the pivot position and runs a curve, takes on the crossing of 4, and dynamically runs to the right, towards the goal (F). If 4 remains defensive, 6 makes a jump shot at the goal (H).
- 4 moves to the 6-meter line after the pass and places a screen on the inner side, next to 2 (G).

- If ④ prevents the shot, ⑥ passes the ball into the running path of ⑤ (J).
- ⑤ does a dynamic piston movement towards the gap between ⑤ and ⑥, and tries to break through (K).
- If ⑤ and ⑥ close the gap and hence make breaking though impossible, ⑤ passes the ball to ③ on the wing position (L) who shoots at the goal (M) or starts a counter piston movement (N).

⚠ Each player should do the piston movement in such a way that he would be able to shoot himself.

⚠ During the initial action on the other (left) side, it might be useful for ⑤ (if left-handed) and ⑥ to switch positions during the normal passing movement (O) so that ⑤ can feint a shot with his left (throwing) hand after the crossing and hence increase the pressure on the defense players (P).

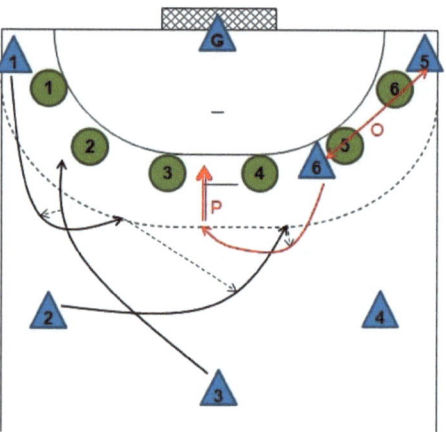

TU 6-7	Final sprint		5	90

Course:

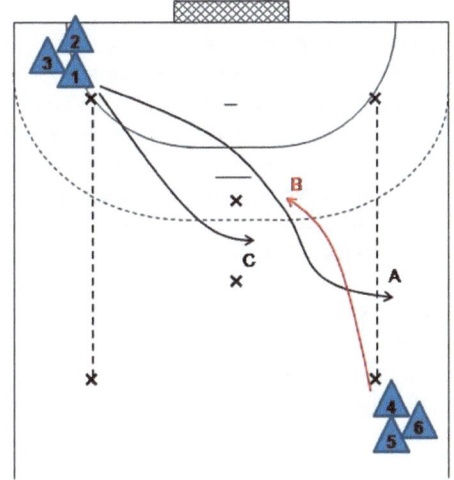

- On command, 1 tries to cross the opposite line, without being touched by 4 (A).
- 4 tries to catch 1 and tag him (B).
- If 1 manages to cross the line without being touched, he gets a point. If 4 touches him before, 4 gets a point.
- Afterwards, 2 starts the same drill. Keep going until all players of the team have done the exercise once. Switch tasks afterwards.
- Which team scores highest? The losing team must do push-ups or sit-ups.
- If 1 takes the longer way through the cone goal and then crosses the line without being touched, he gets two points (C).
- Which team has scored highest after 1 or 2 rounds?

5. About the editor

JÖRG MADINGER, born in Heidelberg (Germany) in 1970

July 2014 (further training): 3-day coaching workshop: "Basic components of goalkeeper training", held by the **German Handball Association (Deutscher Handballbund, DHB)**
Lecturers: Michael Neuhaus, Renate Schubert, Marco Stange, Norbert Potthoff, Olaf Gritz, Andreas Thiel, Henning Fritz

May 2014 (further training): 3-day coaching further training during the VELUX EHF Final4, held by the **German Handball Coaching Association (Deutsche Handball Trainer Vereinigung, DHTV)/DHB**
Lecturers: Jochen Beppler (DHB coach), Christian vom Dorff (DHB referee), Mark Dragunski (coach of TuSeM Essen, Germany), Klaus-Dieter Petersen (DHB coach), Manolo Cadenas (coach of the Spanish national team)

May 2013 (further training): 3-day coaching further training during the VELUX EHF Final4, held by the **DHTV/DHB**
Lecturers: Prof. Dr. Carmen Borggrefe (University of Stuttgart, Germany), Klaus-Dieter Petersen (DHB coach), Dr. Georg Froese (sports psychologist), Jochen Beppler (DHB base camp coach), Carsten Alisch (young talents' hockey coach)

Since July 2012: A-License, DHB

Since February 2011: Handball club trainings, coaching (training and competitive areas)

November 2011: Foundation of the Handball Specialist Publishing Company (Handball Fachverlag) (handall-uebungen.de, Handball Practice and Special Handball Practice)

May 2009: Foundation of the handball online platform handball-uebungen.de

2008-2010: Youth coordinator and youth coach, SG Leutershausen (Germany)

Since 2006: B-License

Editor's note
In 1995, a friend convinced me to join him in coaching a handball youth team (male, under 13 years of age).

This was the beginning of my career as a team handball coach. Ever since I enjoyed working as a coach and had high requirements concerning my exercises. Soon, the standard pool of exercises wasn't enough for me anymore and I started to modify and develop drills myself.

Today, I coach a broad range of youth and adult teams with different performance levels and adjust my training units to the individual needs of the teams.

A few years ago, I started selling my exercises and drills online at handball-uebungen.de. Since, in handball training, there is a tendency towards a general athletic training that focuses on coordination work – especially in the training of youth teams –, a large number of my games and exercises can be applied to other sports as well.

Get inspired by the various game concepts, be creative, and rely on your own experiences!

Yours sincerely,
Jörg Madinger

6. Further reference books published by DV Concept

From warm-up to handball team play – 75 exercises for every handball training unit

By making your training units more diverse, you can increase the players' motivation, since you consistently offer new approaches to improve and refine familiar movement sequences. In this book, you will find inspiring exercises you can apply during each phase of your everyday team handball training – from warm-up and goalkeeper warm-up shooting to the common contents of the main phase and the closing games. Each exercise is illustrated and described in an easy, comprehensible manner. Specific notes give you tips on what you need to be aware of.

This book deals with the following key subjects:

Warm-up:
- Basic warm-up
- Short warm-up games
- Sprint contests
- Coordination
- Ball familiarization
- Goalkeeper warm-up shooting

Basic exercises, basic play, and target play:
- Offense/series of shots
- General offense
- Fast throw-off
- 1st and 2nd wave
- Defensive action
- Closing games
- Endurance

At the end of this book, you will find an entire methodological training unit. The objective of this training unit is to improve shooting and quick decision-making under pressure.

Minihandball training and handball training for young kids (5 training units)

Minihandball training and handball training for kids is different from handball training for older players and considerably different from handball training for competitive players. During their first contact with "handball", kids should be familiarized with the ball in a playful way. They should be taught that being active, doing sports, playing together, and even playing against each other is fun.

This book contains a short introduction to handball for kids and young children and its special characteristics as well as example exercises which help to make your training units interesting and more diverse.

Following this, there are five complete training units of different difficulty levels that focus on the basic handball techniques (dribbling, passing, catching, shooting, and defending in a game with opponents). The kids are playfully introduced to the subsequent handball-specific basics. At the same time, particular attention is payed to general physical experience and the development of coordination skills.

The exercises are illustrated and described in an easy, comprehensible manner. They can be immediately integrated in every training unit. By using the given training variants, you can easily adjust the difficulty level of the training units to the respective target group. The variants should also encourage you to modify and further develop the exercises to make each training unit a new and more diverse experience for the children.

Passing and catching while moving – 60 exercises for each handball training unit

Passing and catching are two basic handball techniques which must be trained and improved continuously. These 60 practical exercises offer you various options to train passing and catching in a challenging and diverse manner. The exercises particularly focus on improving passing and catching skills even during highly dynamic movements. The drills therefore combine new running paths and movements similar to real game situations.

The exercises are illustrated and described in an easy, comprehensible manner. They can be immediately integrated in every training unit. Various difficulty and complexity levels allow for adjustment of the passing and catching drills to each age group.

Effective goalkeeper warm-up shooting – 60 exercises for every handball unit

Goalkeeper warm-up shooting is essential for almost every training unit. These 60 warm-up shooting exercises provide you with a variety of ideas to make the warm-up shooting challenging and diverse, both for the goalkeepers and the field players. The exercises particularly focus on improving the players' dynamics even during the warm-up shooting.

The exercises are illustrated and described in an easy, comprehensible manner. They can be immediately integrated in every training unit. Whether you combine the exercises with additional coordination drills or use them as an introduction to the main part – various difficulty levels allow for adjustment of the warm-up shooting to each training unit and age group.

Competitive games for your everyday handball training – 60 exercises for each age-group

Handball needs quick and correct decisions in each game situation. This can be trained playfully and diversely through handball-specific games. These 60 exercises are divided into seven categories and train the playing skills.

The book deals with the following subjects:

- Team ball variants
- Team play with different targets
- Tag games
- Sprint and relay race games
- Ball throwing and transportation games
- Games from other types of sports
- Complex closing game variants

The exercises are illustrated and described in an easy, comprehensible manner. They can be immediately integrated in every training unit. Various difficulty levels, additional notes, and possible variations allow for adjustment to each age group.

Paperback from the Handball Practice series (Handball Praxis) (five training units each)

Handball Practice 11 – Extensive and diverse athletics training

Handball Practice 14 – Interaction of back position players with the pivot – Shifting, Screening, and Using the Russian Screen

For further reference and e-books visit us at:

www.handball-uebungen.de

www.ingramcontent.com/pod-product-compliance
Lightning Source LLC
Chambersburg PA
CBHW041803160426
43191CB00001B/25